When I Flew

Poetry of darkness and light

by
Gary A. Lucero

This book is dedicated to my late parents. They always provided strength, love, and kindness, even when I disappointed them, which was often. I miss them both, and though I strive to be as patient and hard working as they were, I know I fall short.

This is a work of fiction. Names, characters, places, and incidents are the product of the author's imagination or are used fictitiously. Any resemblance to actual persons, living or dead, events, or locales is entirely coincidental.

Copyright © 2024 Gary A. Lucero

All rights reserved. No part of this book may be reproduced or used in any manner without written permission of the copyright owner except for the use of quotations in a book review.

gluceroo@gmail.com

https://www.garylucerowriter.com

Amazon ASIN: B0CY9FWCCJ

Maxleafsoft

2024

Table of Contents

The Fallen Ones	4
Belief	6
I Do Not	8
End It Stays	10
Life Then Ends	12
Writers of Storm	14
Lightness Round	17
The Unknown Race	19
No Hope	22
Wonder Frail	24
Nothing	26
Subsistence	27
To No Longer	29
When I Flew	31
A Fallen Victim to the Lost	33
She Claims	35
Dead Soul	37
Sacrifice	38
Hopeless	40
In The Twilight	41
Life is Short	42
Come What May	43

In Letting Go..45

The Fallen Ones

We fell below the surface of the sun

Our skin was burning

Our minds were seared

And our hearts lost all hope

Then the wondrous one, she who is mighty

Came riding through the valley of Tunundrom

Crowned in glory, her sword brazen and long

And in moments she swept us to comfort

But the lights in her eyes weren't right

And the feelings we felt weren't true

And before we knew it, she'd gone

And we were left all alone

In our despair we saw it

That our hope had failed us

That our savior was not to be

And that we were indeed lost

Belief

Shine in, happy sojourn

Tides we go, tides we win

And yet we see it

And feel it again

The light, it takes us

The clouds, surround us

And water falls

Falls all the day

So, we see, we live

In life, we give

And chance would have it

And chance removes it too

So, we're left, we fly

Strangers daring, escaped

We soar to heights unknown

Belief that propels

I Do Not

Cascading sacrifice, sorrow, sighs
Darkness fills and light subsides
Mindless worries, sickness seeps
While in loneliness I weep

Barren creation, nothing left
A soul that's empty, bereft
Tides no longer turning
A heart no longer burning

And yet I live this death
I die more with my every breath
I quake and shudder and reel
Yet too dead to stop and feel

This is no longer life
And you're no longer wife
Dead to me as I to you

No more do I believe in I do

End It Stays

Life given, end it stays

We're left and unwanted

Tired, exhausted, we give up

Sorrow takes us when nothing else can

Minds alone, cold, unwoven

Tamed through temptation

Standing without reason

And unable to fathom; cannot comprehend

So, wishes for death

God strike me, kill, deal

An end to justify the means

When nothing else can possibly work

There's no light

No tunnel to end

Just vast wastes, carrion crawlers

Feasting upon our worthless carcasses

And so, we scream

Speechless, fragments breaking

Teeth shattered, tongues cut out

Better dead than alive, and yet we cannot die

Life Then Ends

As we circle the drain of our existence

And approach the realm of the dead

As we navigate the pathways of life's excesses

We see the signs of our sickness

We try to cast our gaze above us

Beyond the dimness of our domain

Straining to find some hope

Some shimmer of light and forgiveness

But our eyes are old and worthless

Unable to focus on anything that lingers

Unable to find hope where none exists

And unwilling to stir the heart

So, we fall deeper into sorrow

Deeper into the realm of the dead

Deeper into the nights of eternity

And slip past the pale into oblivion

With nothing left and no one to help us

With all eyes turned towards the darkness

With all hearts hardened and broken

Life then ends

Writers of Storm

Magical adventures

Great holidays

Lost in the forest

In unmarked graves

Whitewashed but soiled

Reptilian clones

Invading our countries

Our lives and our homes

Wandering pragmatists

Censored though proud

Spouting collusions

But never out loud

Rifled infantry

Stolen from abroad

Shooting at peasants

With nary a job

Man on the street

Drones in the sky

Raining down terrors

That seduce and divide

And mangled monsters

Whose teeth glitter white

Listen in on phone calls

In the dawn an' twilight

Malevolent Masters?

Or scum sucking whores?

They preach from the pulpit

They walk on all fours

They lie and cheat

They collect money for fun

They tell us of freedom

While pointing a gun

They sell us our souls

They guide us to doom

They give us no answers

They build us a tomb

They ride in their limos

They sit in white houses

They carry the plague

Like little shy mouses

And yet they do glitter

They look bright and so warm

They're nothing if not

The writers of storm

Lightness Round

The light of youth

The yearning

The transient expectation

The beginning of beginning

And, with it, angst

Forward march and backwards progress

Never relenting

Always searching

But although the want moves onward

The light can't catch

The narrow ridge of time

It spills and tails round

And darkness enters

Forever rearing it's unwanted head

Forever searching

To bind and to foil

To find and forget

Until some age of maturation

And then things settle

And time slows

The light gathers

The mind clears

And the yearning slows to a crawl

The Unknown Race

I'm not who I'm supposed to be
You've never seen my face
You've never even known me
I am an unknown race

My family's all forgotten
My friends have disappeared
My past is purely nothing
My heart's filled with fear

So why am I still writing?
Is it time for me to flee?
Move beyond this world
To where I can look and see

Try to remember life
Move time that's standing still
Venture beyond this realm

So, I can finally feel

Find a country and a home
And someone to love and hold
A place where peace exists
Where I can grow old

Then death will one day come
And finally, I'll be free
No longer hidden away
Laid out for all to see

My life finally remembered
My face known at last
My soul unencumbered
My soul free to pass

No Hope

In the champaign of death we find our bodies strewn

Lying in a pale bath of piss and shit and blood

With open wounds and fallen souls

With no hope of light

We soldier on as is our way

Oblivious to our current state

Never conscious of our own deaths

Unwilling to admit defeat

As we reach the end of the lonely road

With shadowy figures awaiting our arrival

Solemn glances receive us

And realization arrives

This is the end

No more chances at redemption

Only oblivion and perdition

Damnation without end

That death should be without meaning

A life spent without purpose

A soul lost without reason

It's fitting but unwelcome

Wonder Frail

Frail, light

We soldier on

Tired we stay

More so to stand

And alone we fight

Relentless it seems

A starlight at dusk

And falter we not

And so, he said

"Candles burn,

Both ends be bright,

And yet the shadows do not fall,

They prevail"

But this is life

It lasts but an inst

And never tells it's end

Always in wonder

So, we wait

Lying cold beneath the stones

Our eyes vigilant

Our hearts open

And our minds keen

Waiting for the morn

When fires burn off the cold

When light returns

And our life with it

Nothing

The morning dew was sweet

It was lying on the leaves

The fog was hangin' in the breeze

And the frogs shouted 'cross the lake

Then the missile struck the hill

Fell wildly down and drew

Millions died and so did you

Silence washed us all away

Away went all the memories

In shards of broken light

Then in hell came the night

And the night turned to day

Subsistence

A subsistence of half-truths and petty lies

Of unfulfilled emotions

Of failed expectations

And of constant, never-ending disappointment

A subsistence of underwhelming performance

Of missed opportunities

Of oppressive depression

And of ill-conceived and poorly executed, half-assed attempts at living life

A subsistence of squandered resources

Of poor bargains

Of wasted breath

And of a basic failure to comprehend what's required to exist

A subsistence of mind-numbing stupidity

Of wrong conclusions

Of missed conversational cues

And of a total lack of wisdom and no intelligence at all

To No Longer

To cast myself aloft

To fly and plummet

To glide towards mother earth

To be gripped by fear

To feel the wind whip and tug and tear

To see the ground as it rises up to meet me

To lose all hope

To know the end is near

To realize it's almost over

To crash and be crushed

To lie in a heap, alone and dead

To wipe the slate clean

To loose my soul from the cares of this earth

To severe myself from my family

To never again worry

To no longer fear

To no longer love

To no longer hate

To no longer

When I Flew

When I flew through the window

Lights taped to my armpits, slowly burning

Mice skittered to and from

And yet you sat stammering

When I flew through the archway

Jesus hanging from my feet

You laughed, callous in contempt

And yet he was not amused

When I flew through the air

Sights set on star systems unseen

You couldn't judge the navigational inputs

And I crashed and burned

When I flew inside the Earth's core

My eyes watering from the elements

And I found the item you had lost

You never thanked me on its return

And so, I flew through the escape hatch

My mind's eye otherwise preoccupied

As water passed below me

You could care less, even had you tried

A Fallen Victim to the Lost

you walk alone, the brightness shimmering

you stumble forward, unsure of your next steps

then your vision darkens, fading light and memories

and then blackness, as you see the veil draw near

the images come, as your breath fades away

and in the darkness, the light slowly returns

and as you walk, she is standing there

a ghostly image, translucent in serenity

it's a migrant farmer's widow, a lost and twisted soul

she is no one, and everyone and all

she stammers, still and quiet echoes fading

her eyes pierce yours, and you turn away

you shutter, the vision flickers in the shadows

then she turns, and heads for the burning fields

you wonder still, pondering what and where you are

the light then gathers, and the mist descends again

there are moving passages, and calls to other days

wanton memories, of missing scenes and patterns stilled

you venture forth, but you never see the same again

you wake from dreams, of time and space surreal

blinking still, you think of her and strain

was she real, and who was she again?

a living being, a fallen victim to the lost

a trampled foreigner, she was and could never be

She Claims

As she opens to accept the offering

Young and bright and eager to achieve

As she tugs at his bones and skin

As she washes him

As she covers him

As she swallows him

As she makes him her own

Not a willing subject

But a captive one

As she forms him anew

No more man and no more earth

Just a part that nourishes her

He improves her

And so, death folds in on him

And life springs within her

The continuity of it all proceeds

Another falls victim to the recurrence

Another light extinguished

Another hole filled

Another claimed by her

Another claimed...

Dead Soul

You stand next to me

Yet I'm alone

No warmth nor softness

No comfort, no love

I know we used to be

Loving, light, embers

Souls twined together

But now torn apart

I'm cast aloft

Flying towards the nether

Hurled at light speeds

Dying as I fall

Your hands can't catch me

Your eyes don't see me

Your heart doesn't love me

And your mind knows me not

Which leaves me alone

Floating without life support

Oxygen failing

And lungs collapsed

Sacrifice

I sacrificed my life on the altar of fidelity

A slow death of the flesh

Abstaining to protect integrity

And to guard the sanctity of marriage

My eyes wandered while my body stood still

I craved what I would not have

Always dreaming but never touching

Not even a single word out of place

It's unclear why I waited so long

To whose benefit has it been?

Our love has not grown stronger

Abstinence has not the heart helped at all

And yet I've stood firm and unerring

Always hoping for I know not what

Always with wandering eyes

And an ever wandering heart

Hopeless

I'm hopeless

With no light

And nowhere to go

And no one to talk to

I wonder

Would she want me?

Would she love me?

Would she see me?

As pain fills the crevices

Shimmied into those spaces left by age

As it tears down the walls

What will be left? Anything at all?

In The Twilight

In the twilight effervescence knell

We stood, lights that shone so brightly

And in standing we knew, soldiers we

Ready to fight and die for our king

In the raging, mangled heap of fire

Dragons' flames licking at our blades

We never doubted nor faltered

We died often, and we died well

In the graves, shallow as they were

Maggots consuming our flesh and bones

We lay, alone and without our maker's breath

Our king but only saddened at our demise

Life is Short

Life's transient

Fleeting at best

A wink of the eye

Proving always our mortality

And though we must continue

We have to struggle

We're always self-aware

Always keen to realize our frailty

Thus we live

Never knowing

Never realizing

But always sure that life is short

Come What May

While some hold on to barely an existence

It's unfathomable to me

To live in death, to wake to darkness

To wander through the graves

I'd rather go

Transition to nothingness

Become ash

Find heaven, hell, or whatever there may be

But so many refuse to

Refuse to find peace and solemnity

Refuse to end their struggles

Refuse to face what's waiting for them

But not me

Once life holds no more pleasures

I'll leap off a building to my end

And if cancer comes a calling

It can take its hold

It can consume me

I'll not overstay my welcome

I'll not be a walking dead man

Let death come when it may

In Letting Go

In feeling emotion

In sensing the patterns of stars and the signaling of twilight

In letting go

In falling faster through a spiraling staircase of dreams

And in finding, finally, something to hold onto

One finds him or herself

Made in the USA
Middletown, DE
20 May 2024

54482915R00029